A N ... ers

DK READERS is a compelling reading programme for children. The programme is designed in conjunction with leading literacy experts, including Cliff Moon M.Ed., who has spent many years as a teacher and teacher educator special ..ng in reading. Cliff Moon has written more than 160 ! .oks for children and teachers. He is series editor to Col ..s Big Cat.

.eautiful illustrations and superb full-colour photographs c .abine with engaging, easy-to-read stories to offer a fresh a ..pr ..ch to each subject in the series. Each DK READER is .. ..nteed to capture a child's interest while developing h .. .er reading skills, general knowledge, and l .. .f reading.

.. five levels of DK READERS are aimed at different r .. ..ng abilities, enabling you to choose the books that a .. ..ctly right for your child:

P .. ..el 1: Learning to read
L .. .. Beginning to read
L .. .. Beginning to read alone
L .. .. Reading alone
L .. .. Proficient readers

T .. ..mal" age at which a child begins
t .. .. can be anywhere from three to eight
ye .. .d. Adult participation through the
lo .. vels is very helpful for providing
e .. ..agement, discussing storylines and
sc .. ..ng out unfamiliar words.

No matter which level you select, you can be sure that you are helping your child learn to read, then read to learn!

LONDON, NEW YORK, MUNICH,
MELBOURNE, and DELHI

Written by Fiona Lock

Series Editor Deborah Lock
Art Editor Mary Sandberg
Production Editor Siu Chan
Production Pip Insley
Jacket Designer Mary Sandberg

Reading Consultant
Cliff Moon, M.Ed.

Published in Great Britain by
Dorling Kindersley Limited
80 Strand, London WC2R ORL

Copyright © 2008 Dorling Kindersley Limited
A Penguin Company

2 4 6 8 10 9 7 5 3 1
DD448 - 1/08

A CIP catalogue record for this book
is available from the British Library

ISBN: 978-1-40533-144-9

Discover more at
www.dk.com

Contents

DK READERS

LEARNING
pre-level 1
TO READ

Snakes
Slither and Hiss

DK

A Dorling Kindersley Book

Hiss!
The scaly snakes
slither here and there.

scales

Look out!

egg

rat snakes

A baby rat snake
slides out of its egg.
Hiss!

tree

tree boas

eye

Look out!
Tree boas keep
their eyes open.
Hiss!

Look out!
Copperheads flick
their tongues in and out.
Hiss!

copperheads

tongue

Look out!
Parrot snakes open
their jaws very wide.
Hiss!

jaws

 parrot snakes

Look out!
Pit vipers bite with
their sharp fangs.
Hiss!

pit vipers

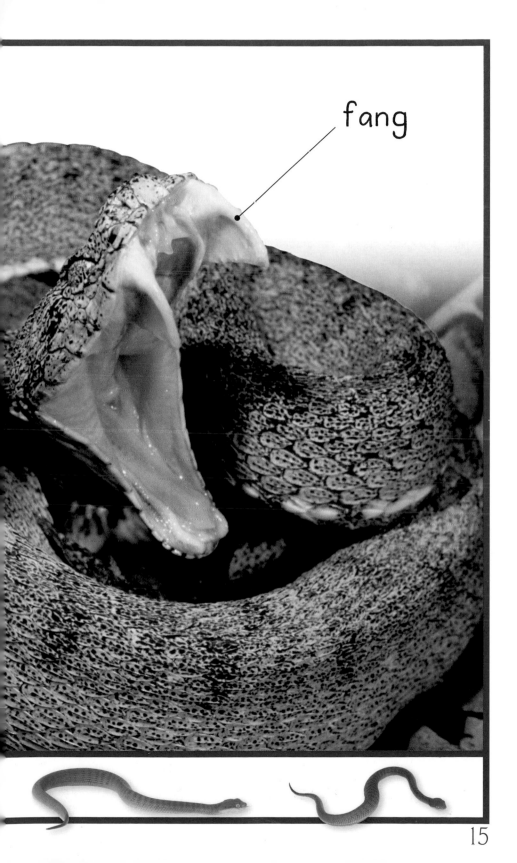

fang

Look out!
Rattlesnakes rattle
their tails when
they are angry.
Rattle!

tail

rattlesnakes

hood

cobras

Look out!
A cobra is getting
ready to spit.
Ssspit!

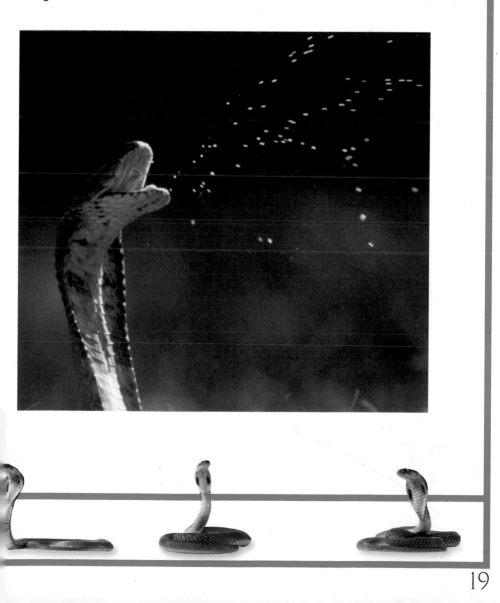

Look out!
Pythons curl
around rats and
squeeze tight.
Sssqueeze!

 pythons

rat

Look out!
Gaboon vipers hide
under leaves.

gaboon vipers

Ssssh!

leaves

snake

Look out!
Sea snakes swim
this way and that.
Ssswish!

sea snakes

stripes

Look out!
Flying tree snakes glide
from branch to branch.
Hiss!

flying tree snakes

branch

body

Look out!
Horned vipers wind
their way across
the sand.
Hiss!

horned vipers

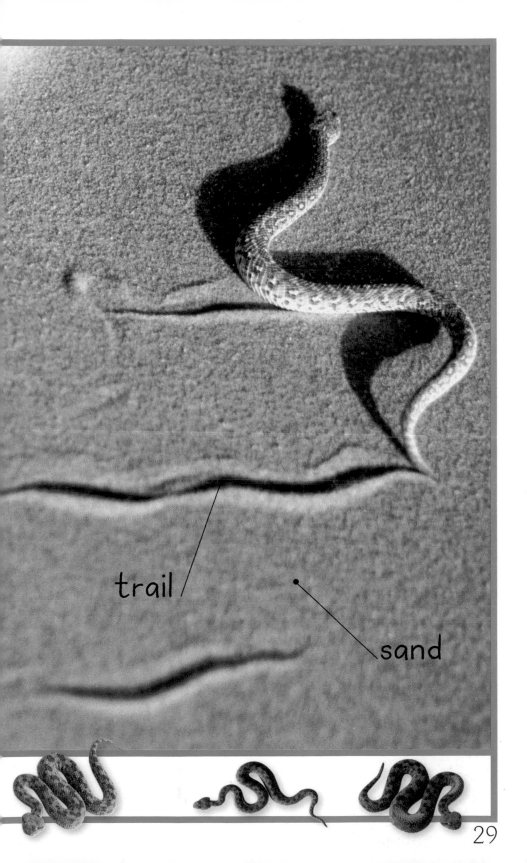

trail

sand

All the sleepy snakes
curl up in coils.
Ssssh!

Can you slither

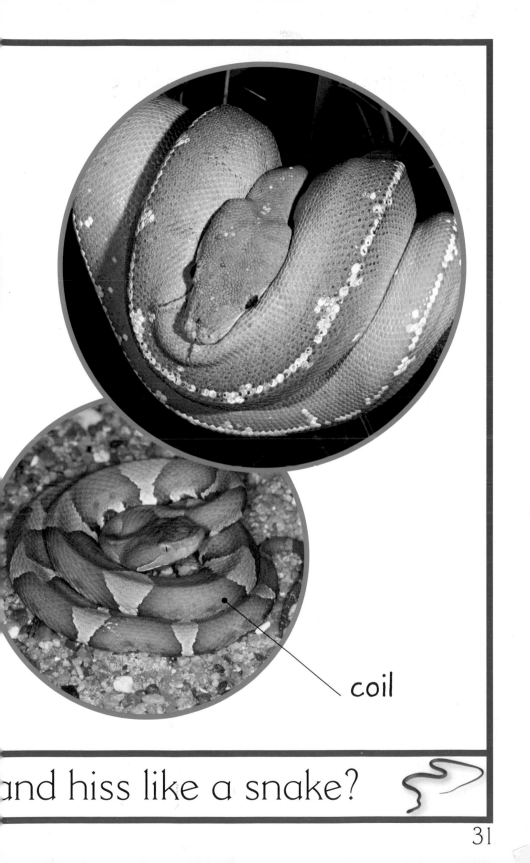

coil

...and hiss like a snake?

Glossary

 **Egg** a soft, leathery shell with a baby snake growing inside

 **Fang** a large hollow tooth that shoots out poison

 **Jaws** bones that open and close an animal's mouth

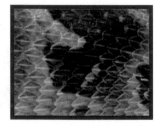 **Scales** small, smooth plates that cover an animal's skin

 **Tongue** a snake's forked mouth part that can smell, touch and taste